SCHIRMER'S LIBRARY
OF MUSICAL CLASSICS

Vol. 2091

OTAKAR ŠEVČÍK

School of Violin Technics
Complete
Parts I-IV, Op. 1

Violin

Edited by Philipp Mittell

ISBN 978-1-4234-9090-6

G. SCHIRMER, Inc.

DISTRIBUTED BY

7777 W. BLUEMOUND RD. P.O. BOX 13819 MILWAUKEE, WI 53213

www.schirmer.com
www.halleonard.com

CONTENTS

PART III: SHIFTING (CHANGING OF POSITION)

PART IV: EXERCISES IN DOUBLE-STOPS

School of Violin Technics
Op. 1, Part I

Erste Lage	First Position
Fingerübungen auf einer Saite	**Finger-exercises on One String**
Man wiederhole jeden Takt mehrere Male, langsam und schnell, gestossen und gebunden, und achte, dass die Finger gleichmässig und fest aufschlagen. Siehe Anmerkung zu Op. 8.	Repeat each measure several times, both slowly and quickly, *détaché* and legato; and be careful that the fingers make the stops evenly and firmly. Read the Remarks at the head of Opus 8.

1.

Edited by Philipp Mittell

Otakar Ševčík
(1852–1934)

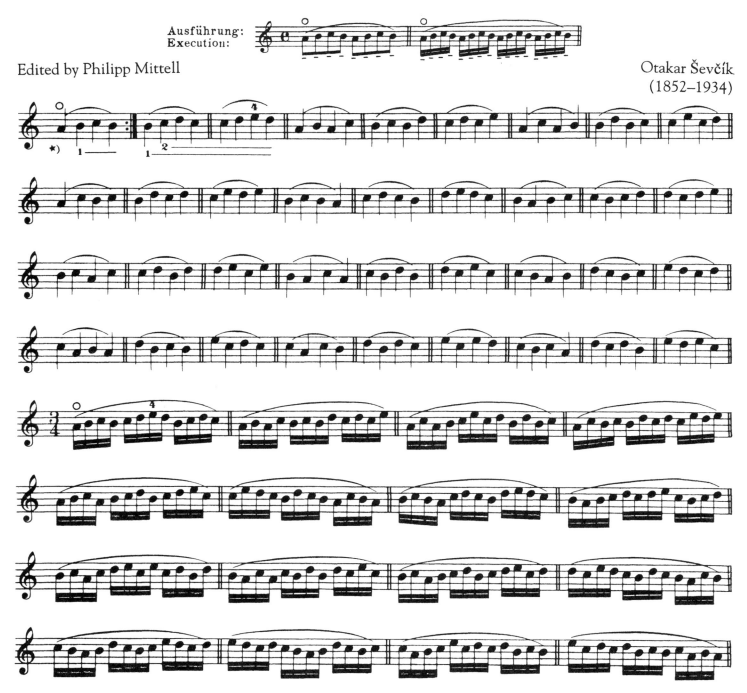

*) Die Finger fest liegen zu lassen   *) Keep the fingers down firmly

2.

3.

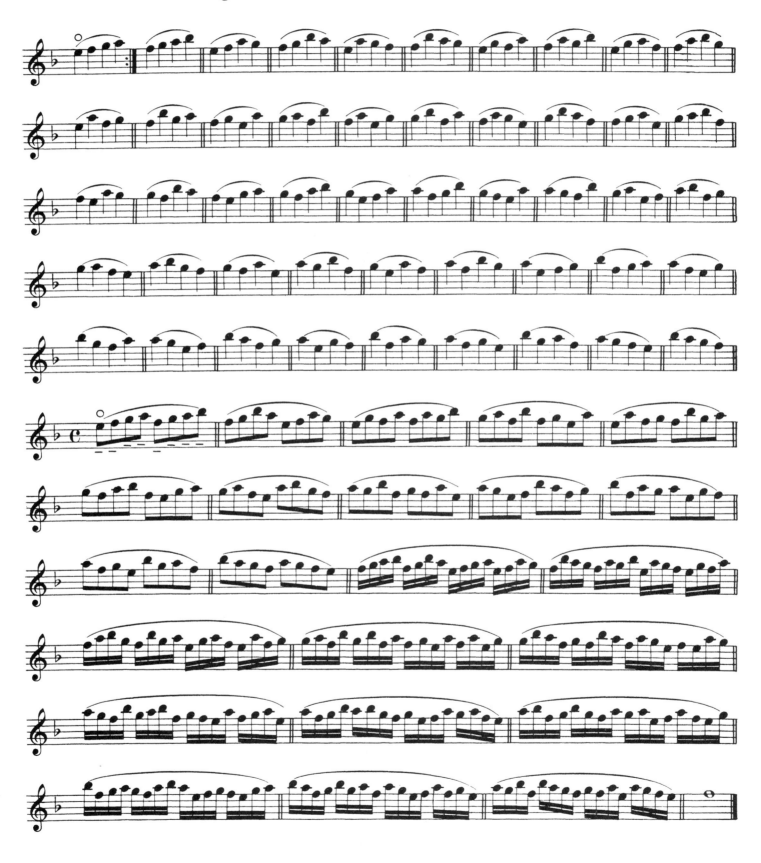

4.

Man wiederhole zuerst jeden Takt einzeln, dann zu zweien.

Repeat each measure by itself at first; then 2 together.

8

5.

6.

7.

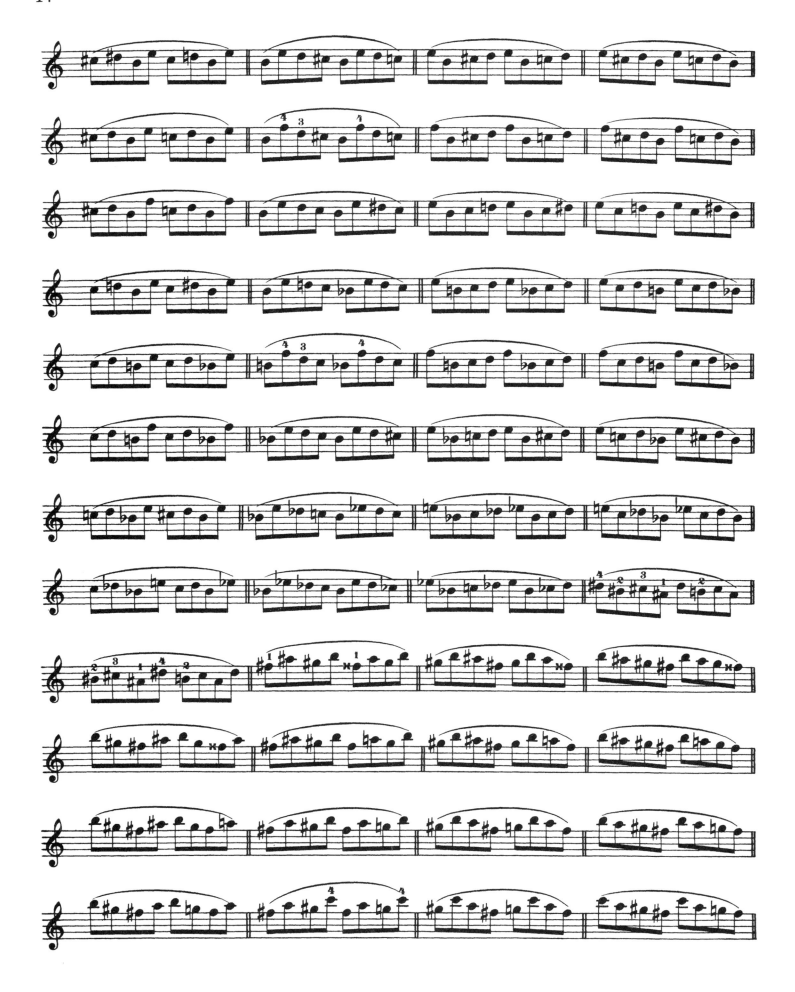

8.*)

*) Diese Übungen sollen **auf jeder Saite** geübt werden. | *) Practise these exercises on each string.

9.

10.

Übungen auf zwei Saiten

Man wiederhole zuerst jeden Takt einzeln, dann zu zweien.

Exercises on Two Strings

Repeat each measure by itself at first; then 2 together.

11.*)

Übung des rechten Handgelenks	Practice for the Right Wrist
Dieses Beispiel ist mit allen folgenden Stricharten auszuführen.	Practise this exercise with each of the bowings marked below.

Beispiel:
Example:

*) Man übe diese Übung langsam in der Mitte, dann erst **an der Spitze** und am Frosch.

*) Practise this exercise slowly in the middle of the bow; after this, at the point and the nut.

Stricharten | **Bowings**

12.

Tonleitern *) | **Scales *)**

*) Auch sind die harmonischen Tonleitern zu üben.   *) Also **practise** the harmonic scales.

13.

Tonleitern in Terzen

Die eingeklammerten Zeichen ♯, ×, ♮, sind nur bei der Wiederholung der einzelnen Moll-Tonleitern zu beachten.

Scales in Thirds

The signs (♯), (×) and (♮) are to be observed only at the repetition of the minor scales.

14.

Übung in Sexten | Exercise in Sixths

15.

Oktaven | Octaves

16.

Nonen, Dezimen u.a. | Ninths, Tenths, etc.

Die Finger sind möglichst lange liegen zu lassen. | Keep the fingers down as long as possible.

17.

Dreiklang   Tonic Triads

18.*)**)

Diese Übung ist mit jeder Strichart ganz aus-zuführen.	This entire exercise is to be practised with each of the given bowings.

Sp.	An der Spitze	} des Bogens.
Fr.	Am Frosch	
G.B.	Mit ganzem Bogen.	

Pt.	Near the Point	} of the bow.
Nut	Near the Nut	
W.B.	Whole bow.	

*) Die Finger liegen lassen.   *) Keep the fingers down.
**) Diese Uebung soll zuerst gestossen geübt werden.

26

19.

Chromatische Tonleiter | Chromatic Scale

20.

Verminderter Septimenakkord

Die ganzen Noten sind zu greifen, ohne gespielt zu werden.

Chord of the Diminished Seventh

Hold down the whole notes without playing them.

21.

22.

Verschiedene Akkorde arpeggirt | Arpeggios of Different Chords

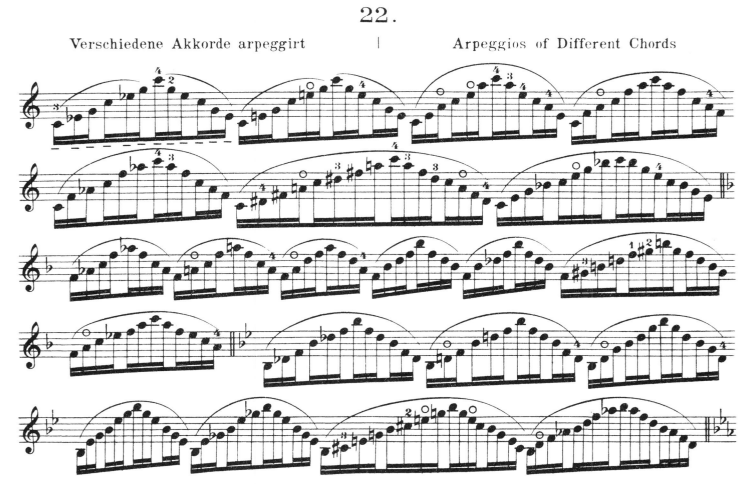

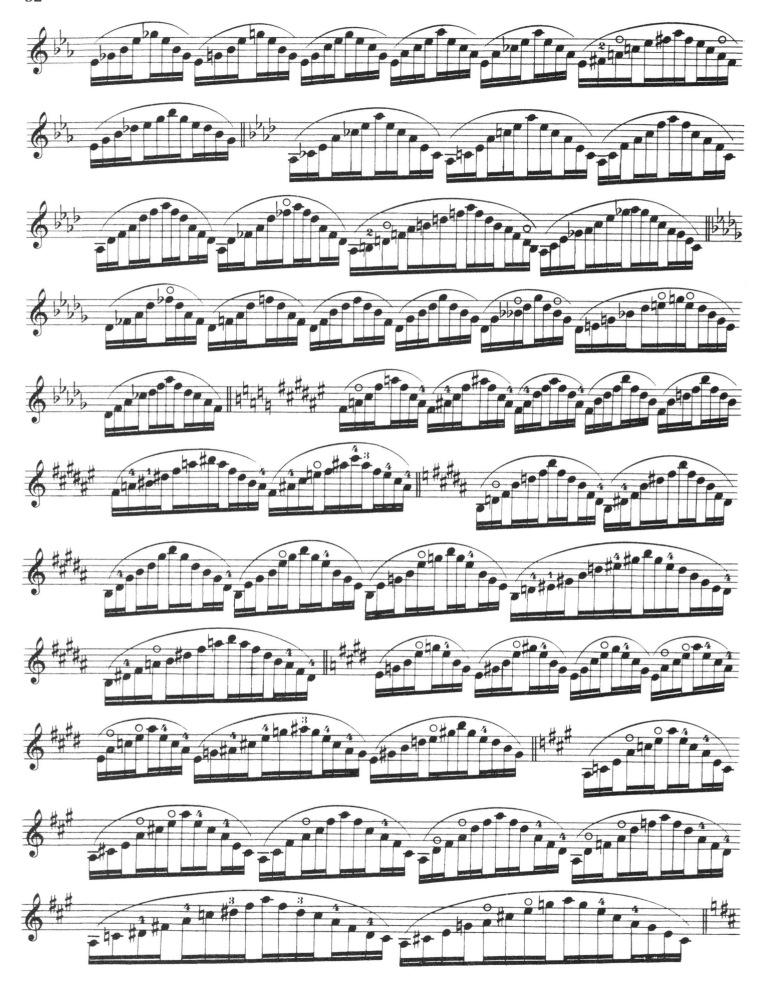

23.

Übungen in Doppelgriffen | Exercises in Double-stops

34

24.

25.

26.

Beispiele in allen Tonarten | Exercises in All Keys

27.

Übung in Akkorden

Exercises in Chords

28.

Dieselbe Übung mit schwierigeren Akkorden | The Same, with more difficult chords

29.

Übung in verschiedenen Stricharten	Exercise in Various Bowings
Erklärung der Zeichen:	Explanation of the Signs.

Sp.	An der Spitze		Pt.	Near the Point	
M.	In der Mitte		M.	Near the Middle	
Fr.	Am Frosch		Nut	Near the Nut	
Fr. z...... Sp.	Vom Frosch bis zur Spitze	} des Bogens.	N. to ..... Pt.	From Nut to Point	} of the bow.
Fr. z...... M.	Vom Frosch bis zur Mitte		N. to ..... M.	From Nut to Middle	
M. z...... Sp.	Von der Mitte bis zur Spitze		M. to ..... Pt.	From Middle to Point	
H. B.	Mit halbem Bogen.		H. B.	With half the bow.	
G. B.	Mit ganzem Bogen.		W. B.	With whole bow.	

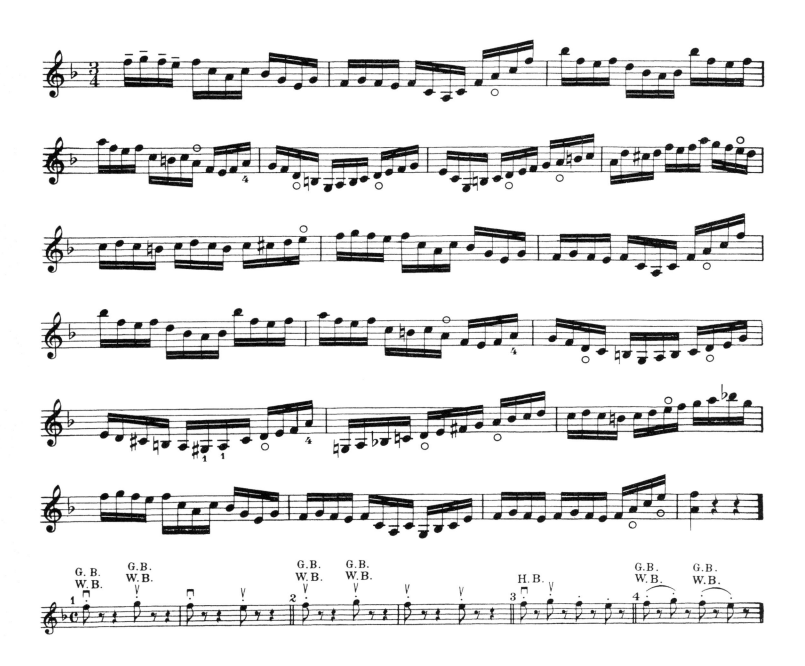

School of Violin Technics
Op. 1, Part II

Exercises in the 2d Position *)

Before taking up these exercises, the student must have
studied op. 8 and op. 9.

1.

Edited by Philipp Mittell

Otakar Ševčík
(1852–1934)

*) Because of their progressive difficulty it is advisable to
practise these exercises in the following order: No. 1, 3-5,
12-13, 15-16, 21, 23, 30, 32-33, 35-36, 39; 2, 6-9, 14, 17-18,
22, 26-29, 31, 37; 10-11, 19-20, 28-29, 34, 38, 40-41.

2.

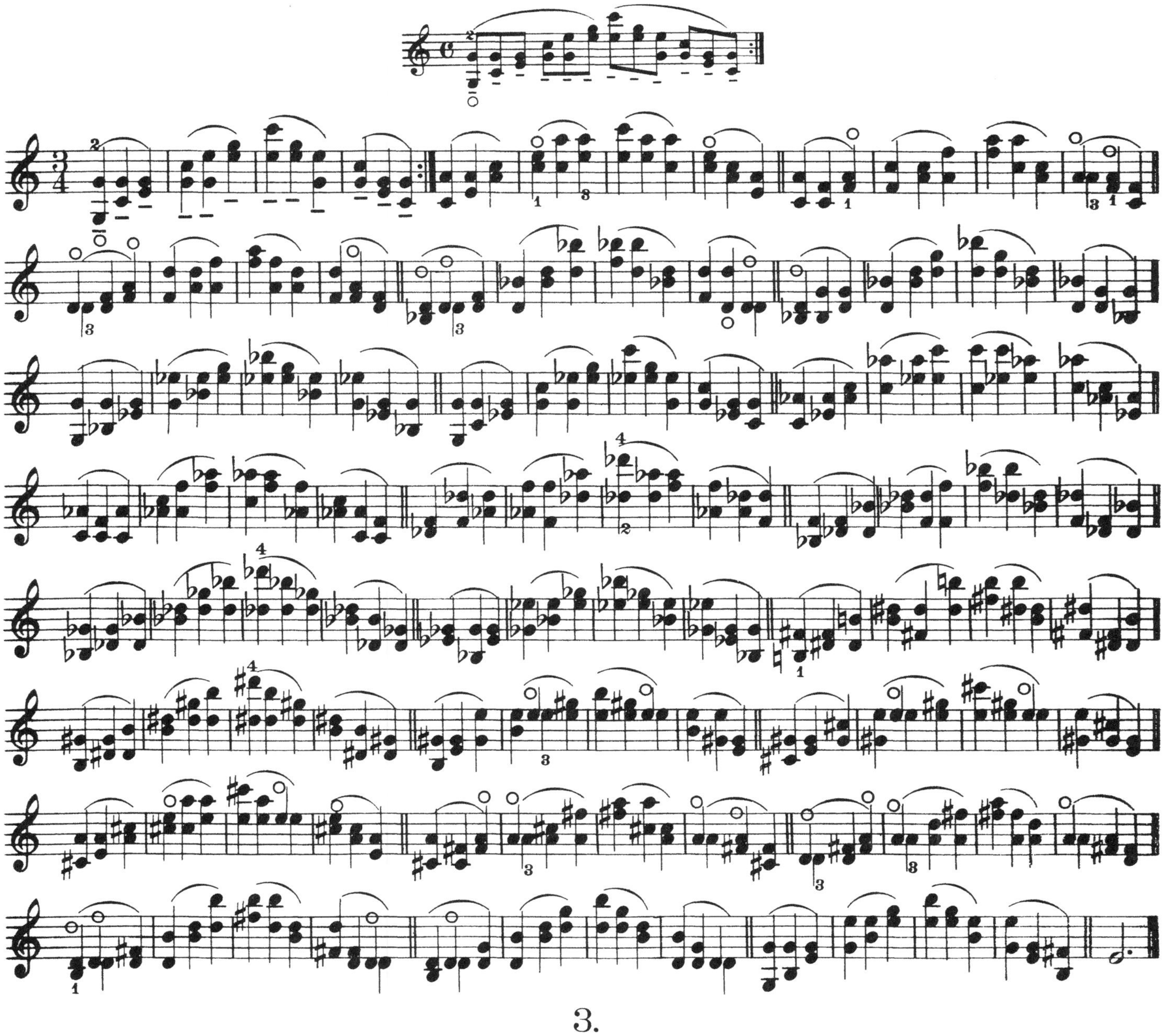

3.

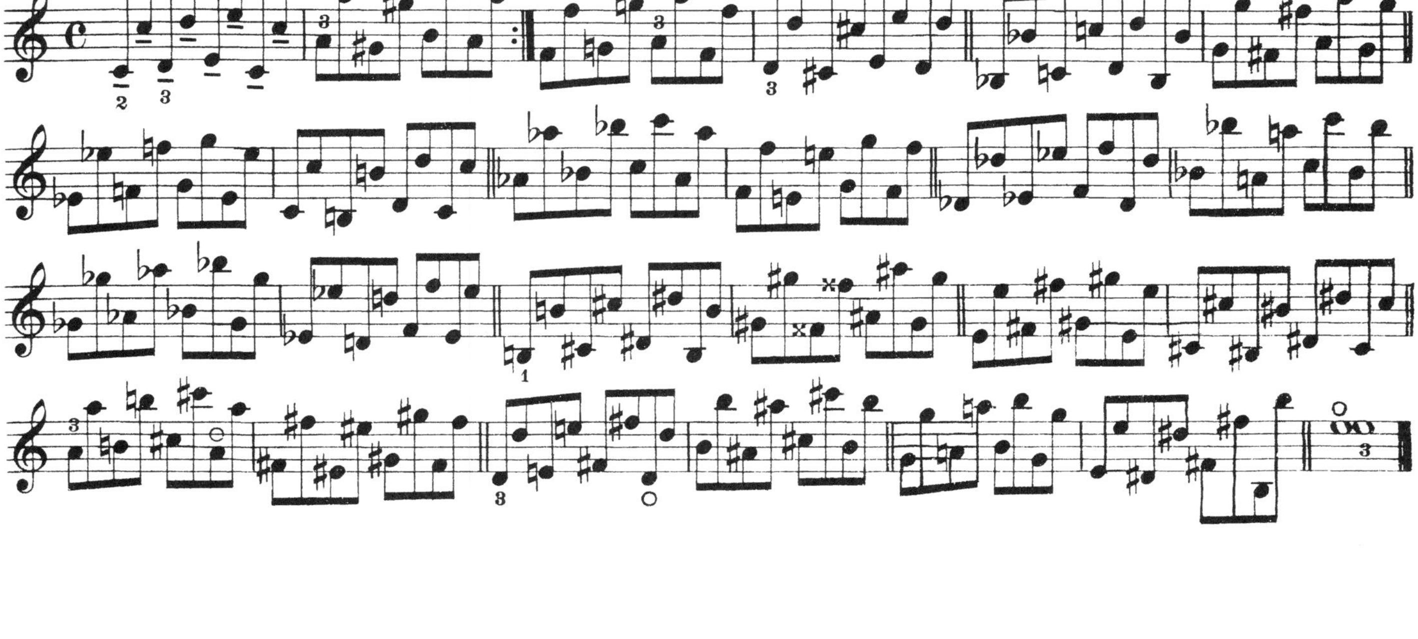

4.

Exercises in the 1st and 2d Positions

5.

6.

Chord of the Diminished Seventh

Hold down the whole notes without playing them.

7.

Exercises in All the Keys

8.*)

Arpeggios of Different Chords

*) Play this same exercise in the 3d and 4th positions.
(See No. 33.)

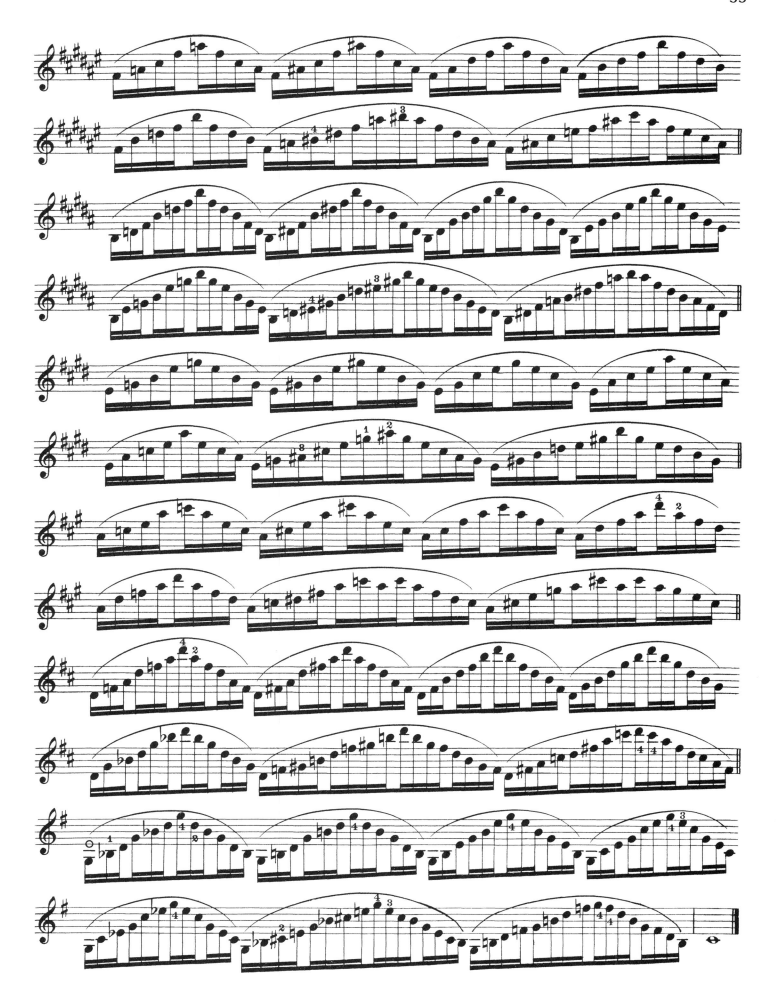

55

56

9.
Chromatic Scale

10.

Exercises in double-stops, in all keys

11.

Exercise on Chords

Notes and chords in small type are to be played by advanced students.

12.

Exercises in the 3d Position

13.

14.

15.

Keep the fingers down as long as possible

64

16.

Exercises in the 1st and 3d Positions

2te und 3te Lage. — 2d and 3d Positions.

17.

Hold down the whole notes without playing them

18.

19.

70

20 *)

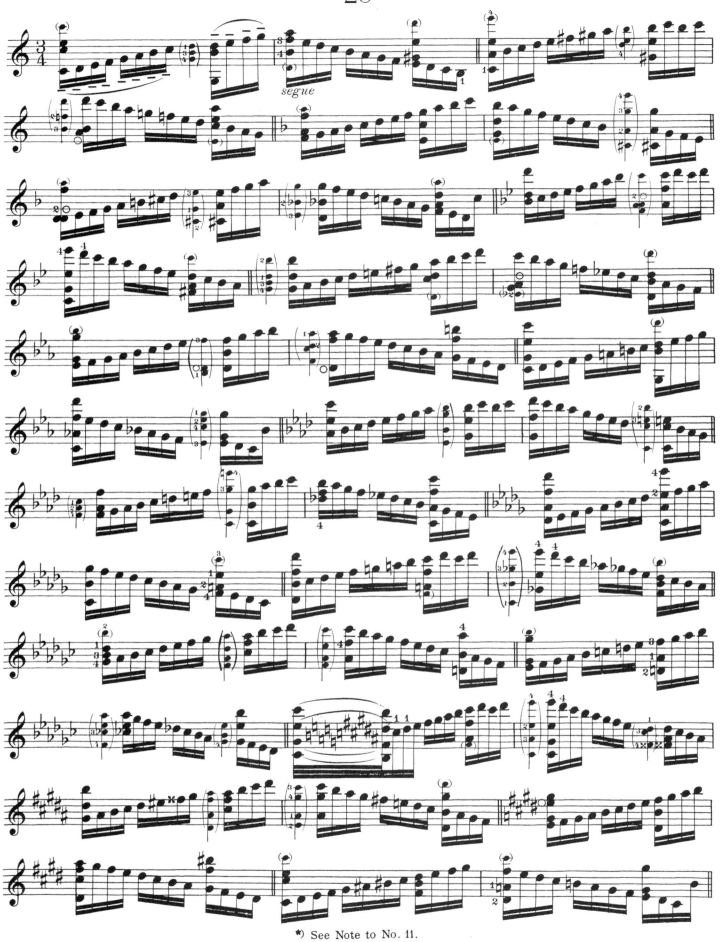

*) See Note to No. 11.

21.

Exercises in the 4th Position

22.

23.

74

24.

Exercises in the 1st and 4th Positions

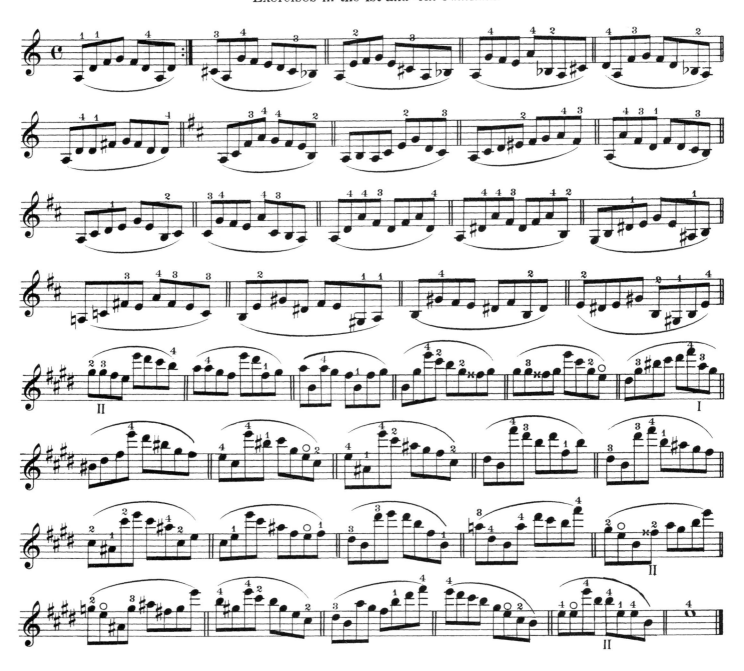

25.

Exercises in the 2d and 4th Positions

27.

28.

29 *)

segue

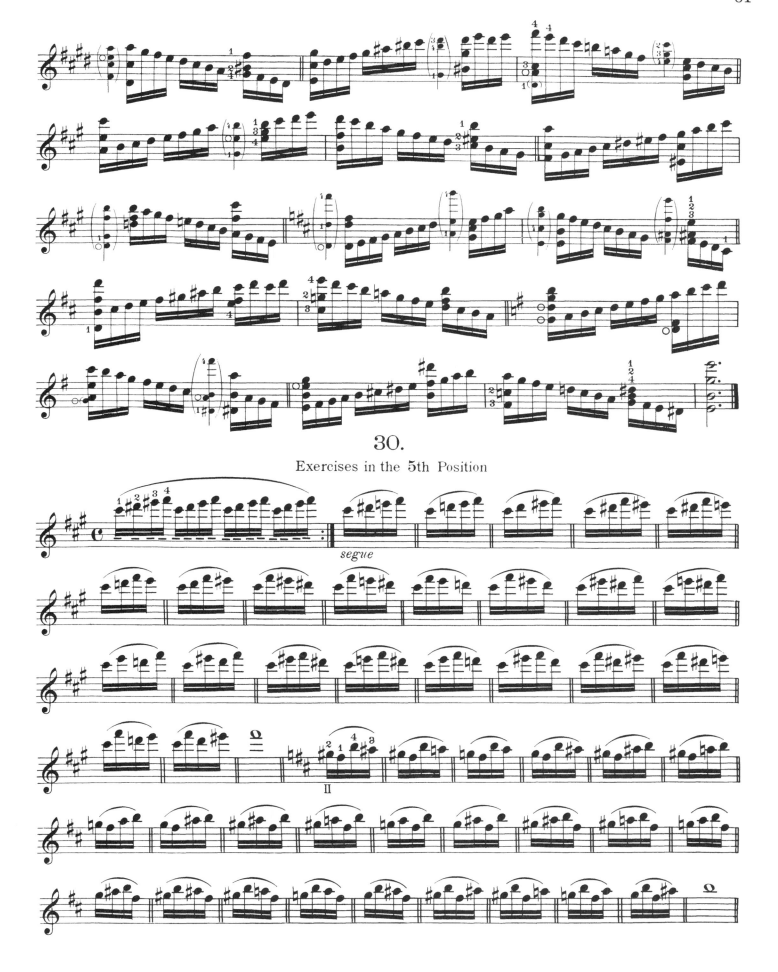

30.

Exercises in the 5th Position

segue

31.

32.

33.

85

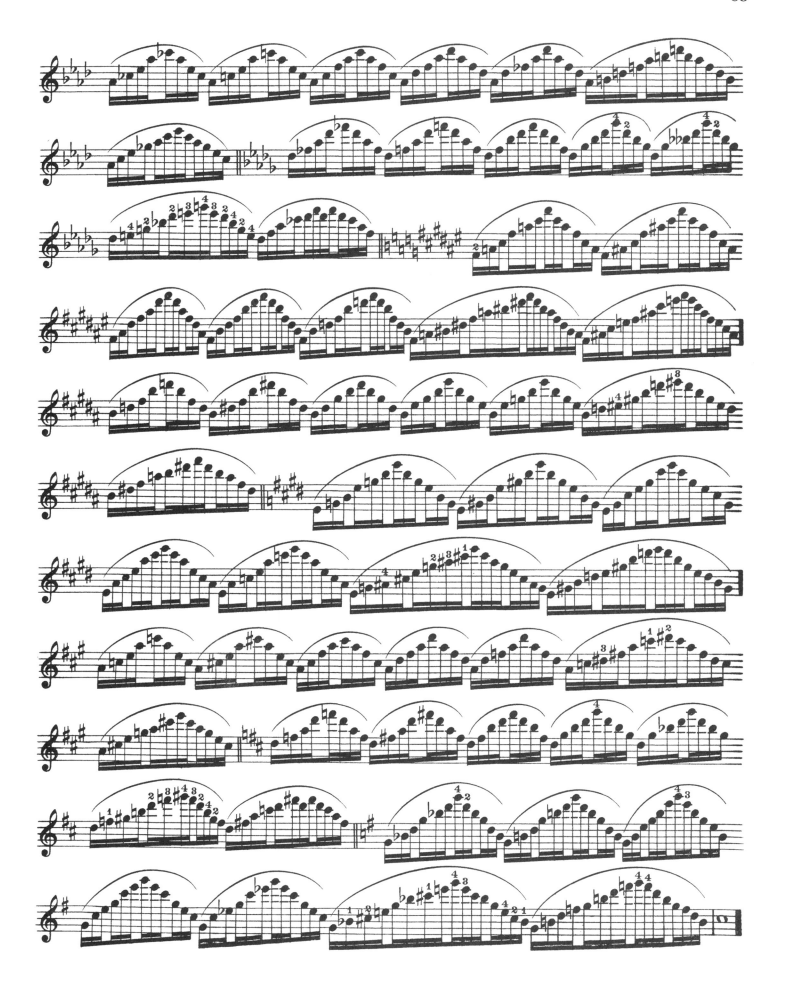

34.

35.
Exercises in the 6th Position

36.

37.

38.

39.
Exercises in the 7th Position

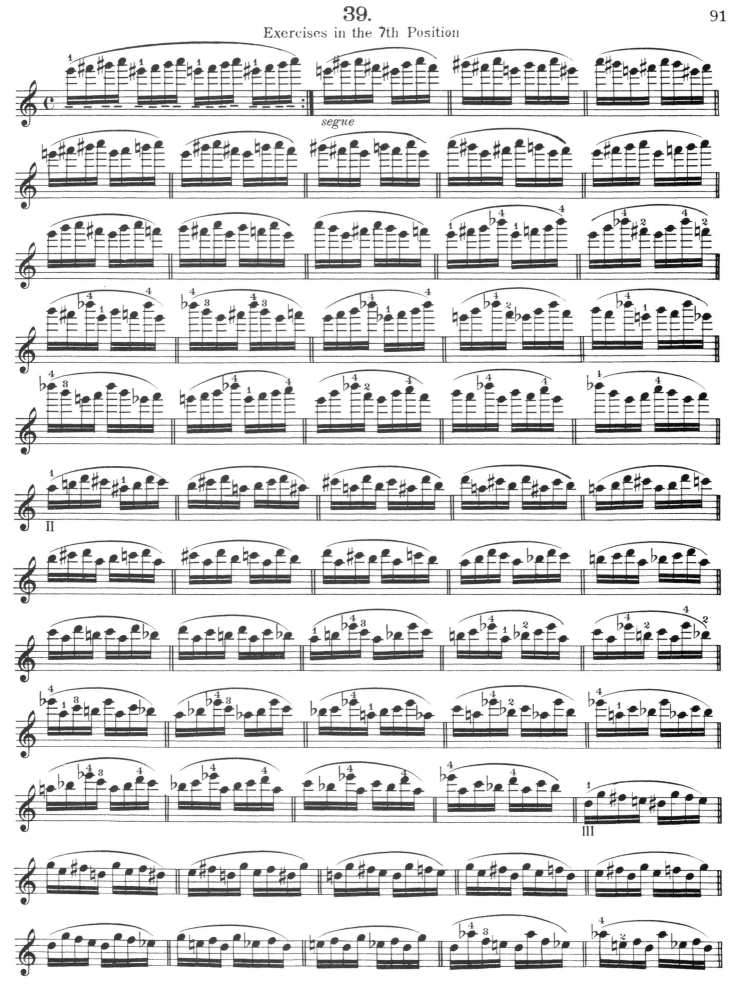

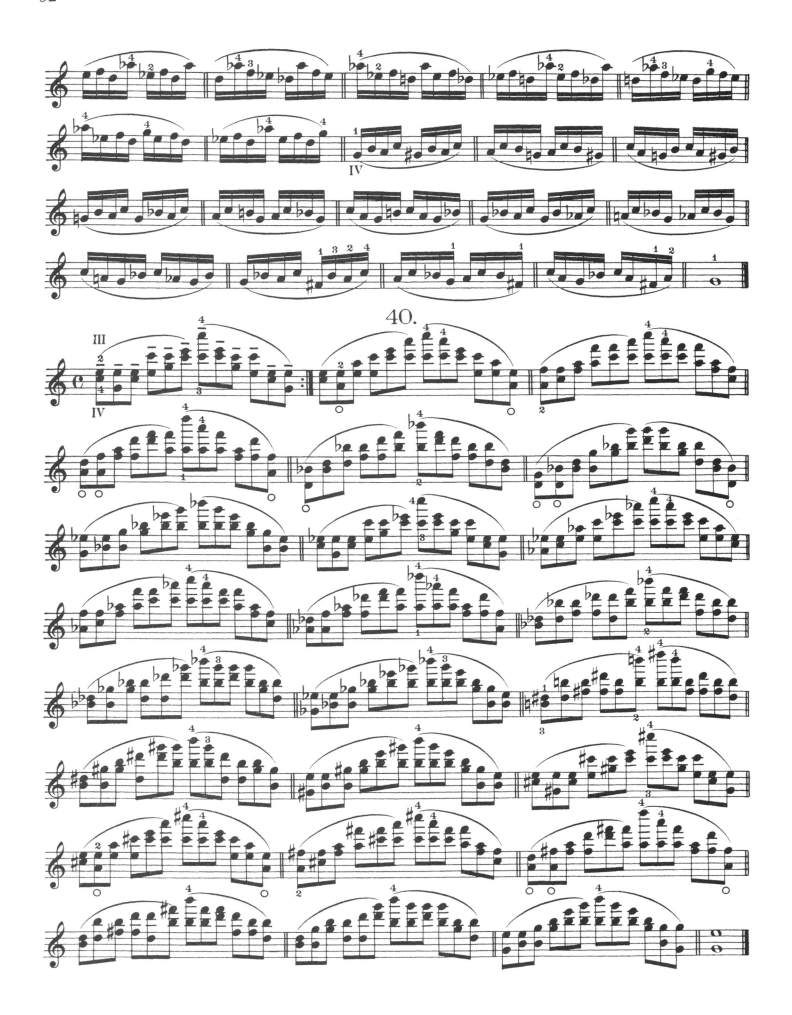

41.

School of Violin Technics
Op. 1, Part III

Lagenwechsel *)

Man übe jedes Beispiel zuerst gestossen und dann gebunden.

Tonleitern auf einer Saite

Edited by Philipp Mittell

Shifting (Changing of Position) *)

Practise each exercise *détaché* at first, and then legato.

Scales on One String

1.

Otakar Ševčík
(1852–1934)

*) Siehe 2ten Teil N⁰ 4, 5, 16, 24, 25.

*) See Part Second, Nos. 4, 5, 16, 24, 25.

Tonleitern durch drei Oktaven   Scales through Three Octaves

2.

Man übe die Tonleitern auch
auf folgende Arten:

The scales must also be
practised as follows:

98

Arpeggien auf einer Saite   3.   Arpeggios on One String

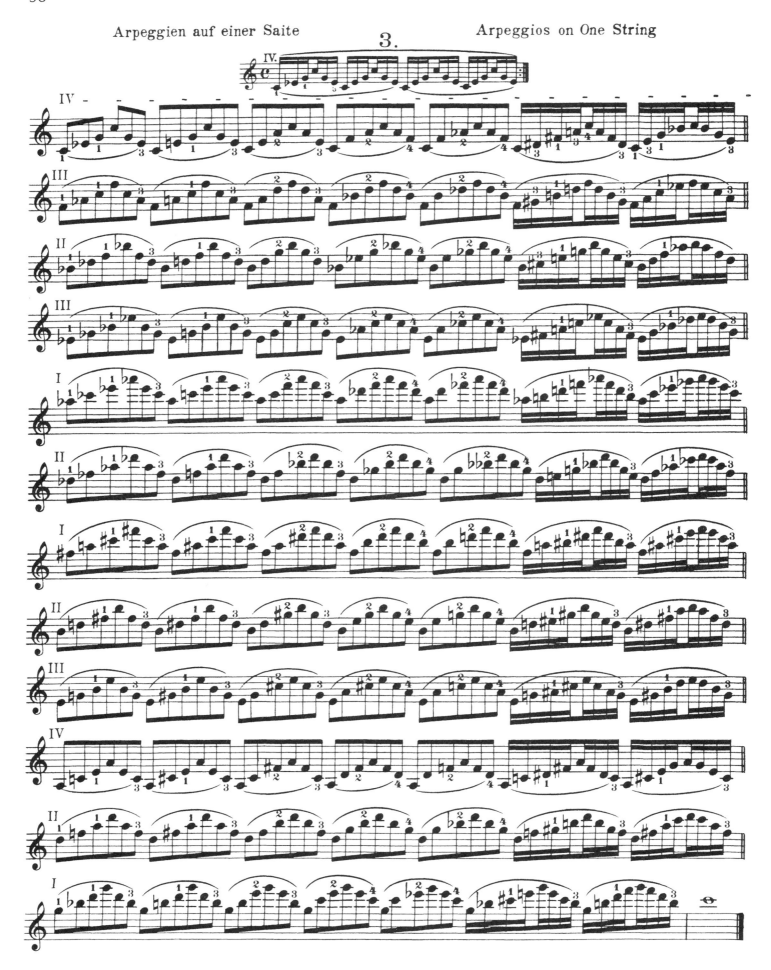

4.

5.

7.

106

Chromatische Tonleiter | Chromatic Scale

8.

Übungen für den Lagenwechsel | Exercises for Changing Positions

9.

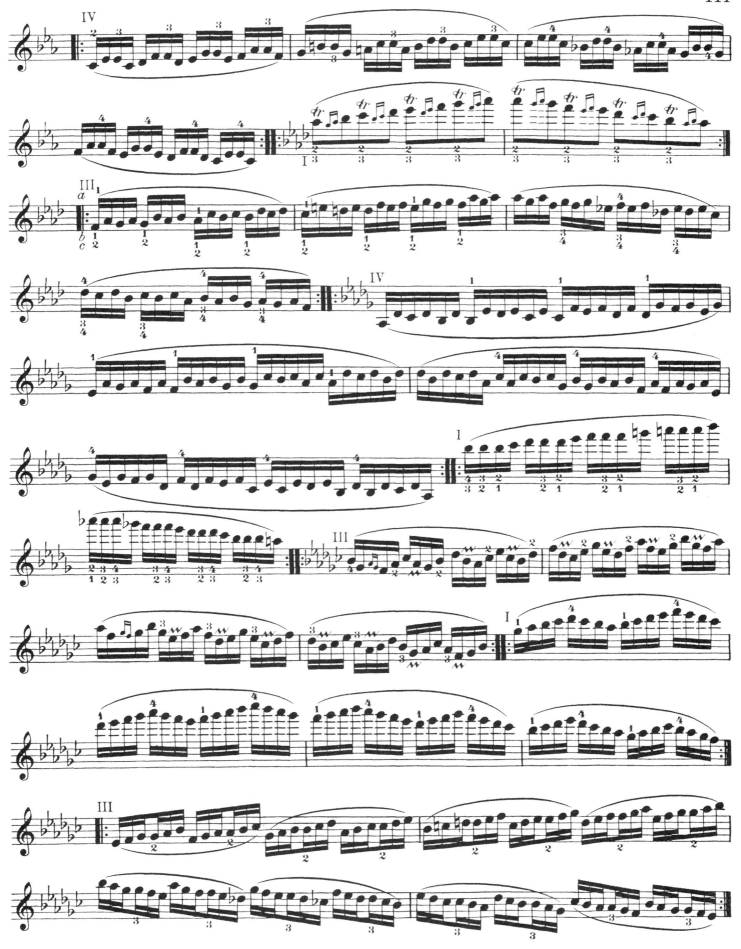

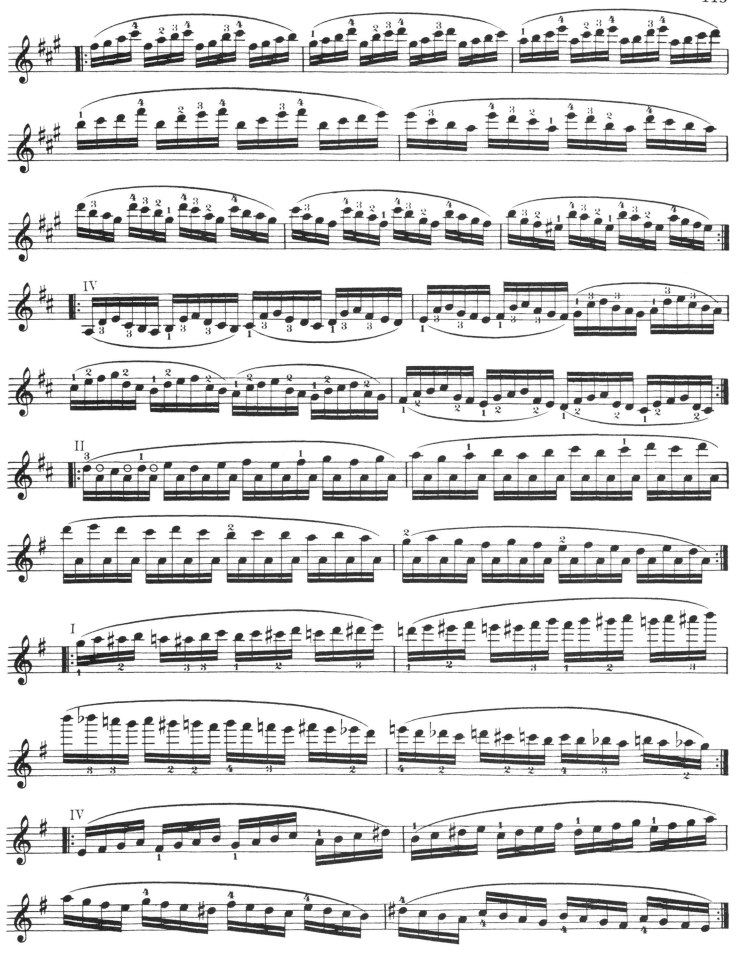

10.

11.

12.

Übung auf der 4ten Saite

13.

Exercise on the 4th String

Diese Übungen sind auch auf der
2<u>ten</u>, 3<u>ten</u> und 4<u>ten</u> Saite auszuführen

14.

Play these exercises also on
the 2d, 3d and 4th Strings

School of Violin Technics
Op. 1, Part IV

Übungen in Doppelgriffen

Gestossen und gebunden zu üben.

Exercises in Double-stops

Practise both détaché and legato.

1.

Oktaven.

Octaves

Otakar Ševčík
(1852–1934)

Edited by Philipp Mittell

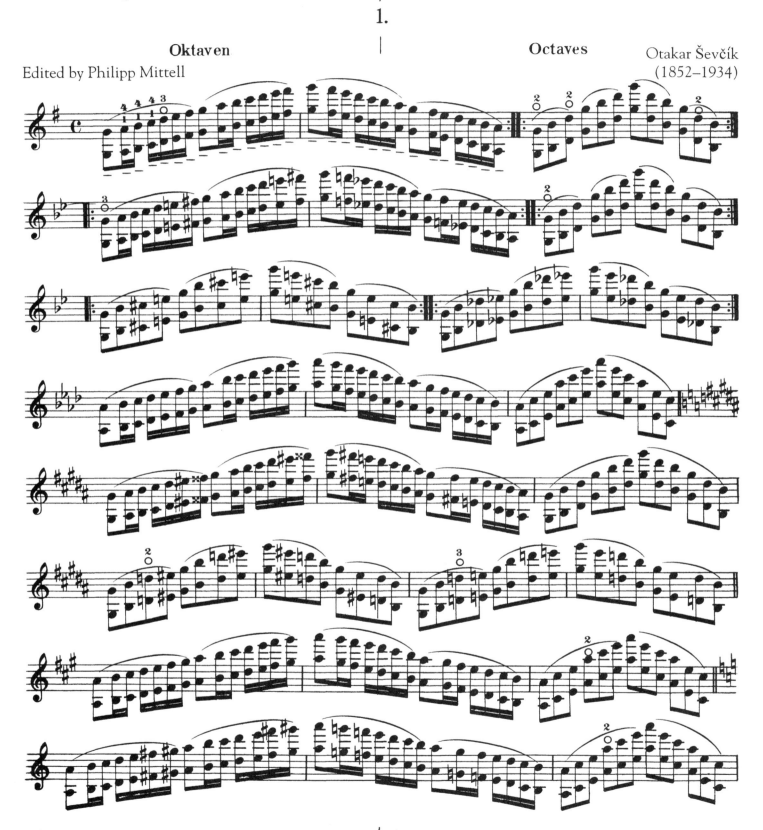

★)Siehe Ersten Teil № 23-26, und Zweiten Teil № 10, 19, 28.

★)See Part First, Nos. 23 to 26, and Part Second, Nos. 10, 19, 28.

123

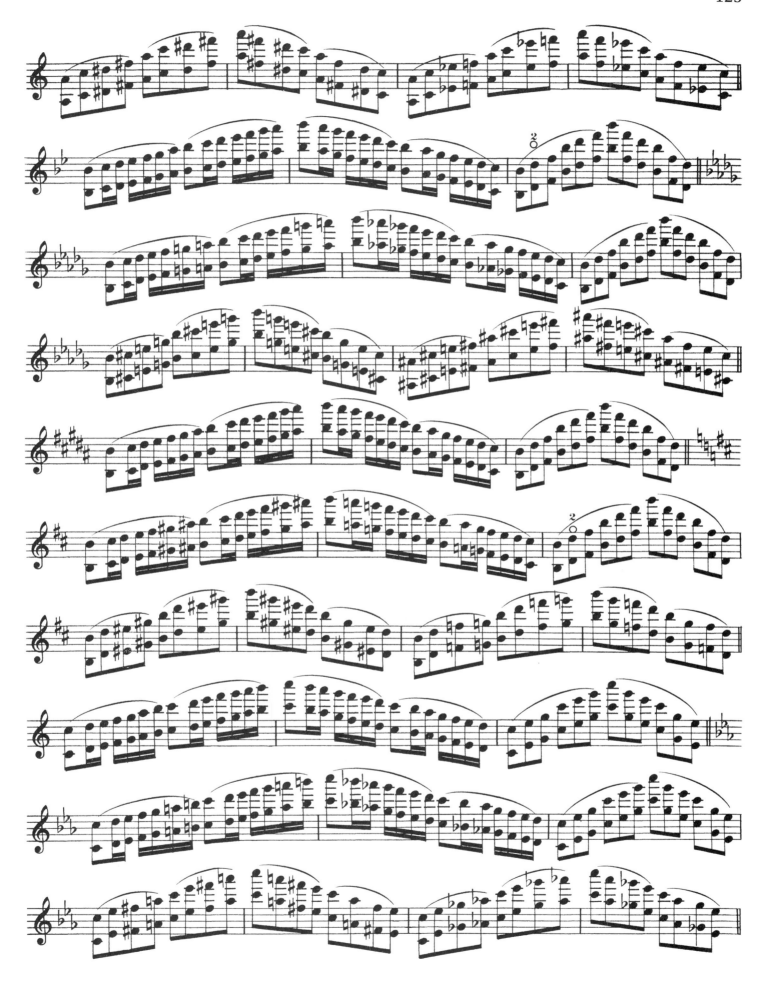

2.

132

5.

Terzen   Thirds

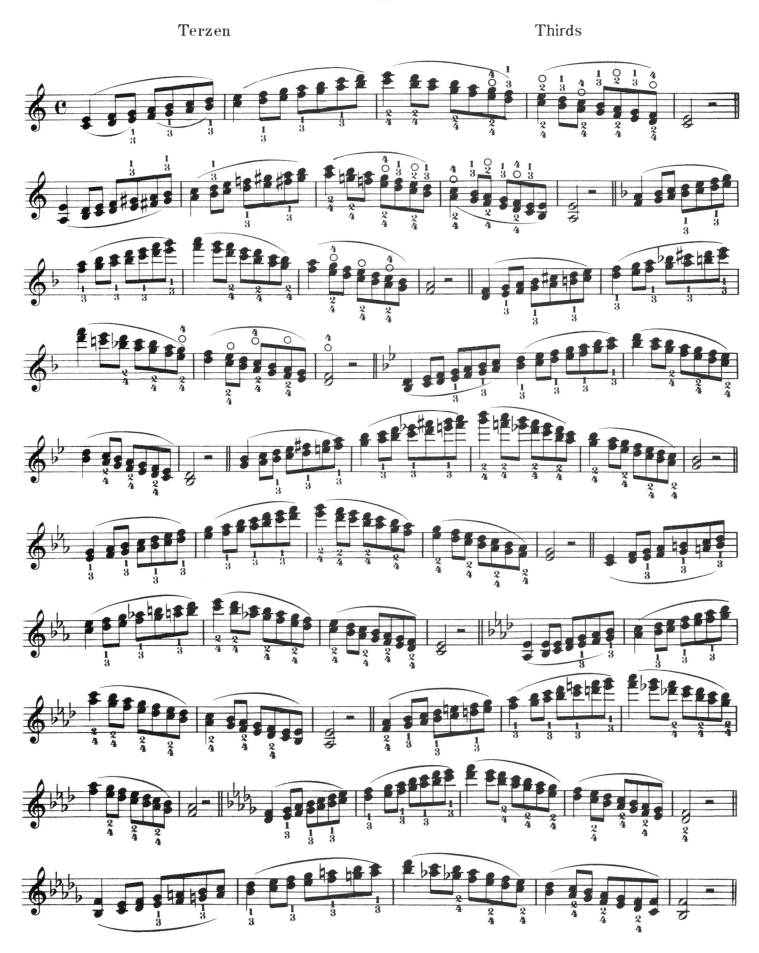

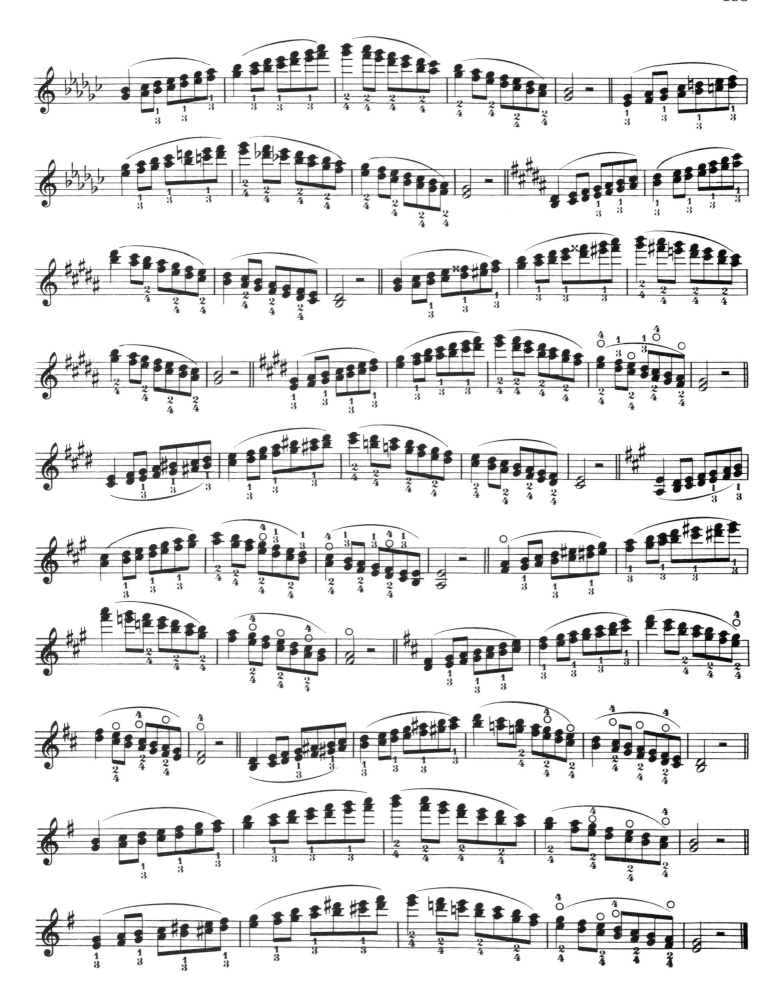

6.

7.

8.

9.

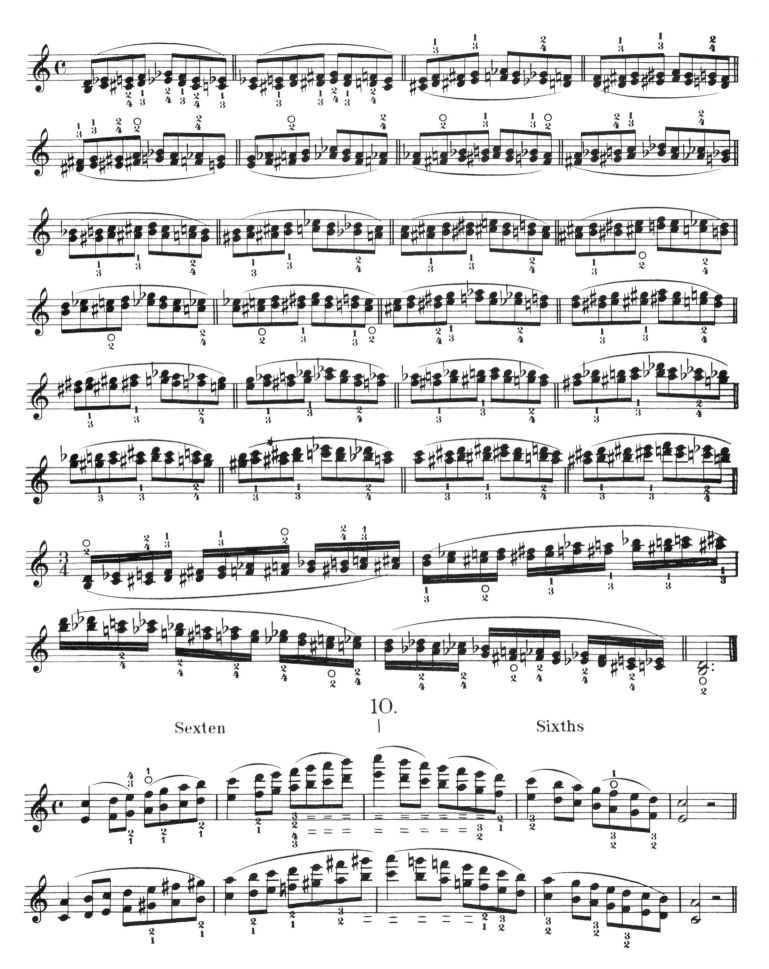

10.

Sexten   Sixths

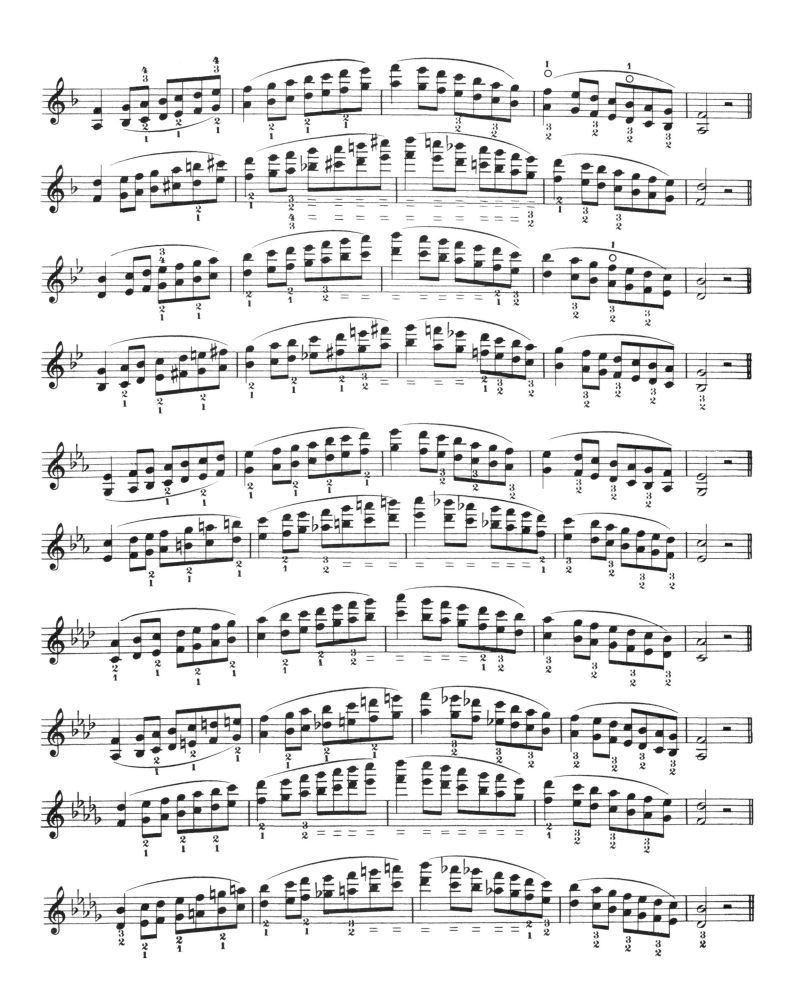

11.

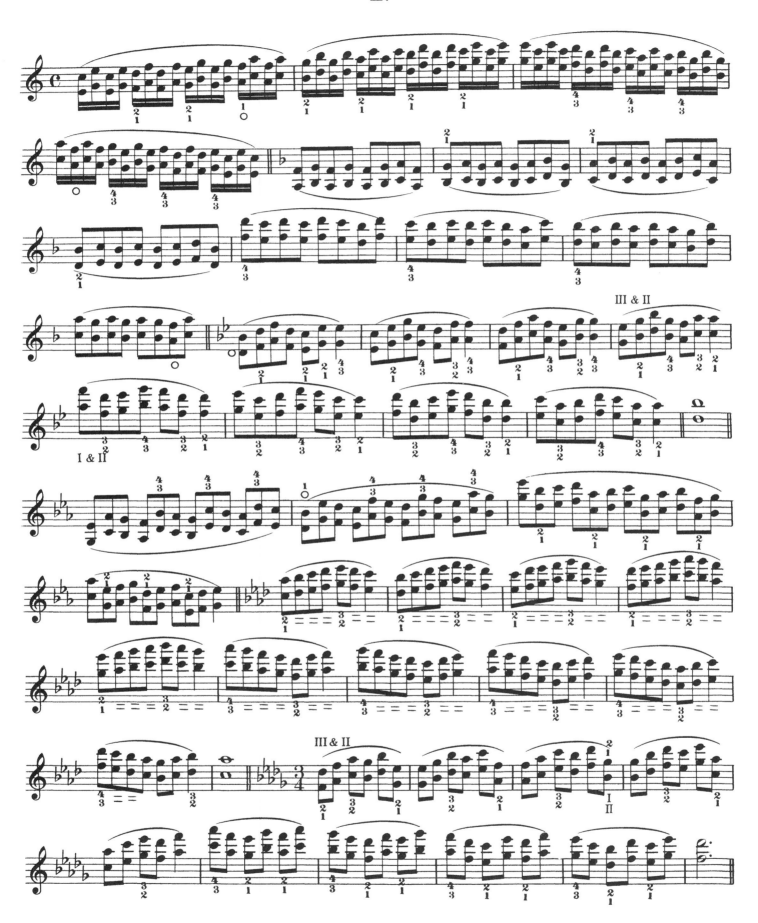

146

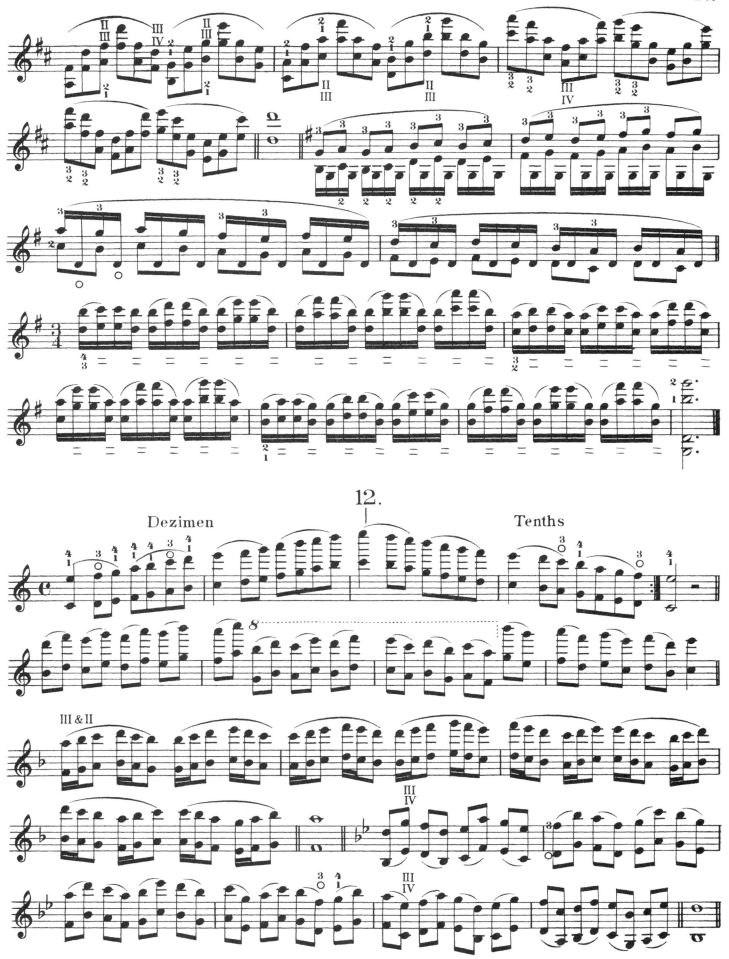

13.

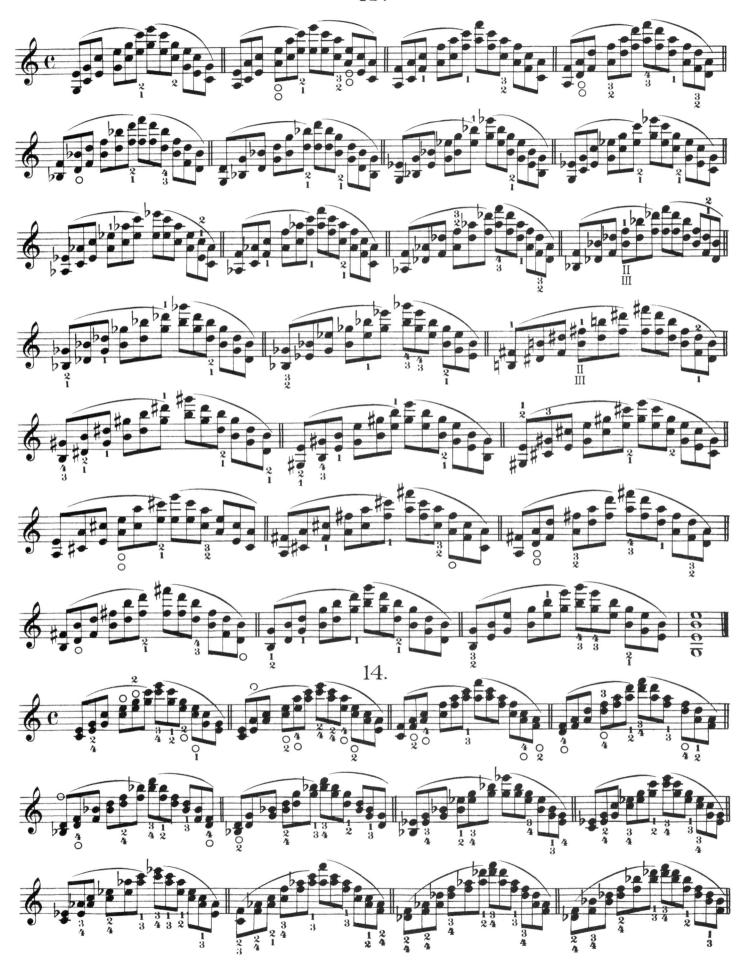

14.

15.

16.

17.

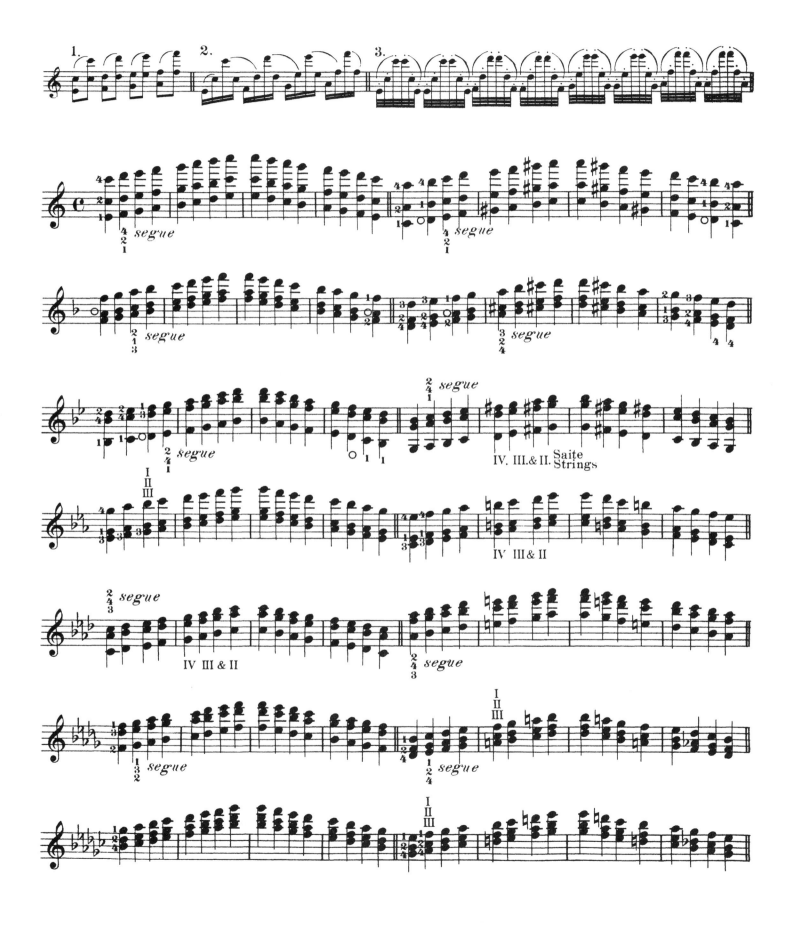

18.

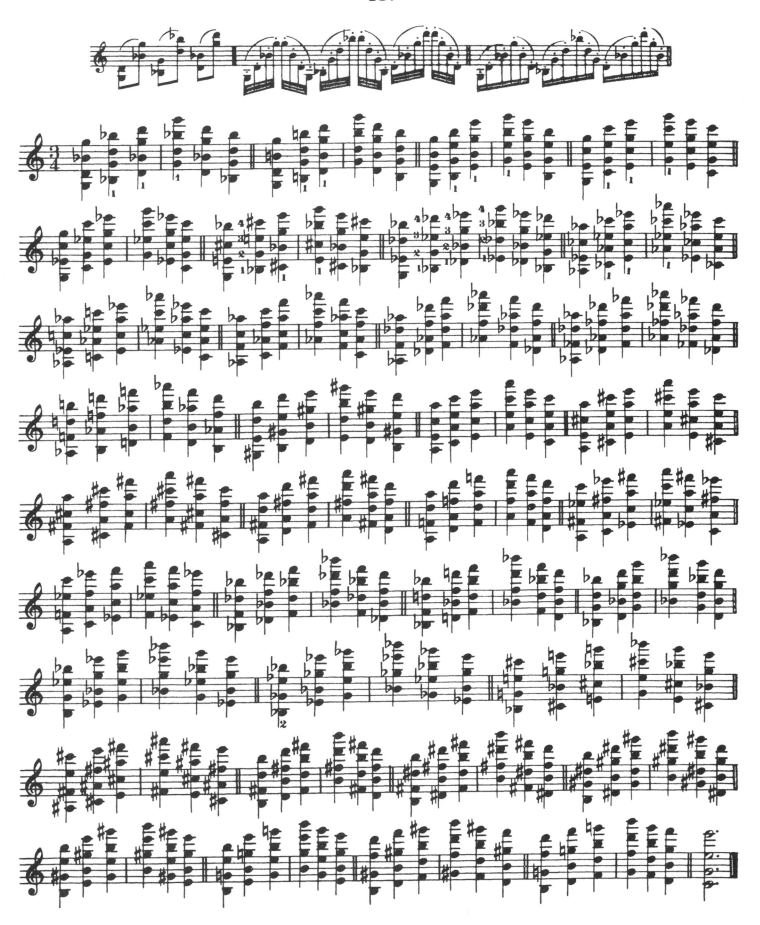

19.

Übungen im Pizzicato
der linken Hand (+)

Exercises on the Pizzicato
for the left hand (+)

20.

Die Finger, mit denen die Saite gekniffen wird, sind mit römischen Ziffern bezeichnet.

The fingers plucking the strings are indicated by Roman numerals.

21.

Übungen in Flageolettönen | Exercises in Harmonics
Tonleitern | Scales

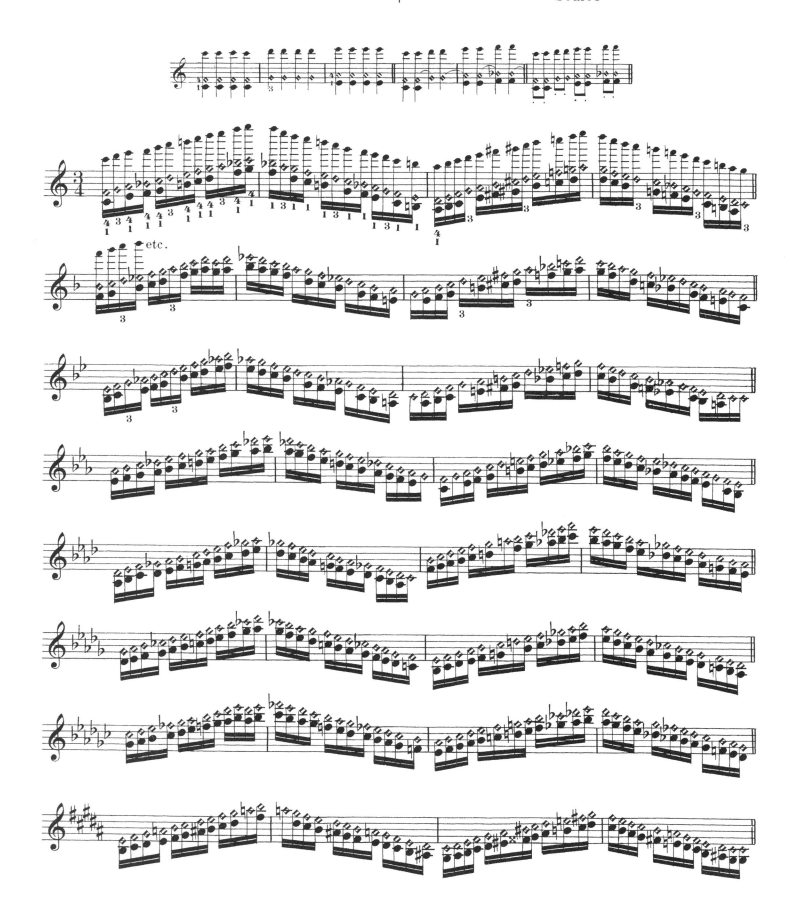

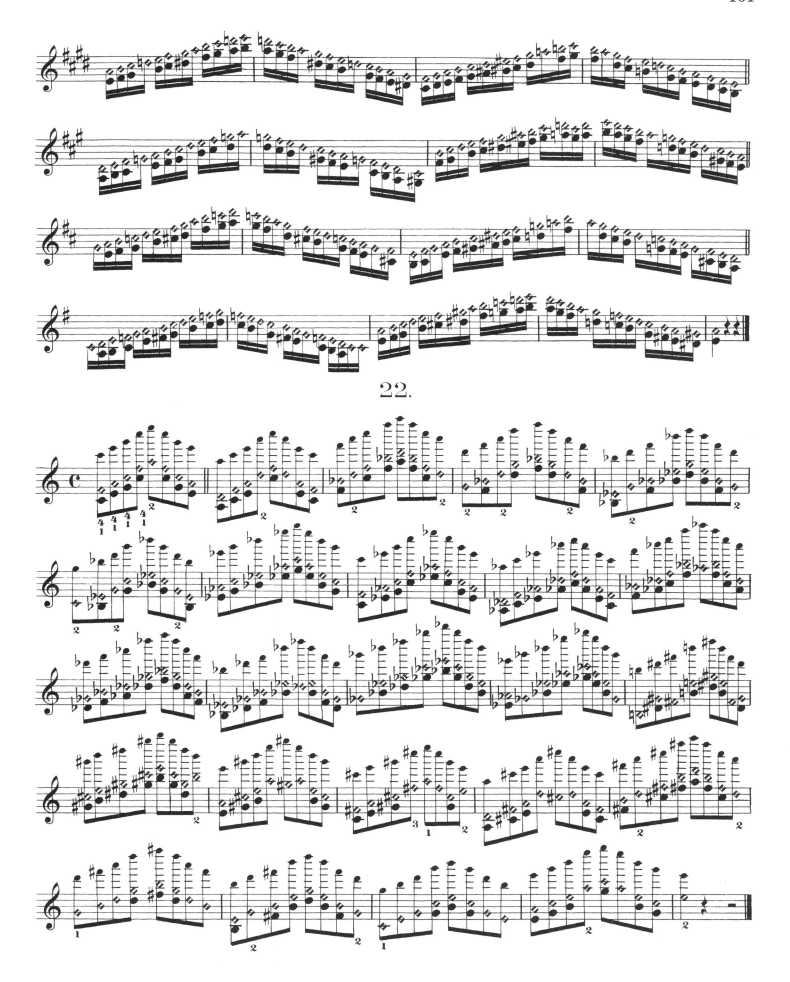

22.

23.

Dur-Tonleitern in Terzen | Major Scales in Thirds

164

In Sexten —In Sixths

In Oktaven —In Octaves

Mischungen von natürlichen und Flageolett-Tönen. | Alternation of Harmonics with stops of regular pitch